Hey, I'm a Story!

Words by Amy Leask

Photos by Octavian Ciubotariu   Illustration by Maria Hurtado

International Standard Book Number: 978-1-927425-21-3

Author: Amy Leask
Photography: Octavian Ciubotariu
Illustration: Maria Jose Hurtado
Design: Maria Laura Hurtado
Editor, Publisher: Ben Zimmer, with special thanks to Karina Sinclair at Line by Line Studio

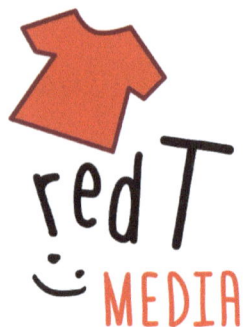

Hey, I'm a Story! first edition published by:
Red T Media,
8560 Tremaine Rd, Second Floor,
Milton, ON, Canada L9T 2X3

www.RedTKids.com

For Yuglis, Manuel, Petru, Constanta, and Dot,
who helped us get to know Story.

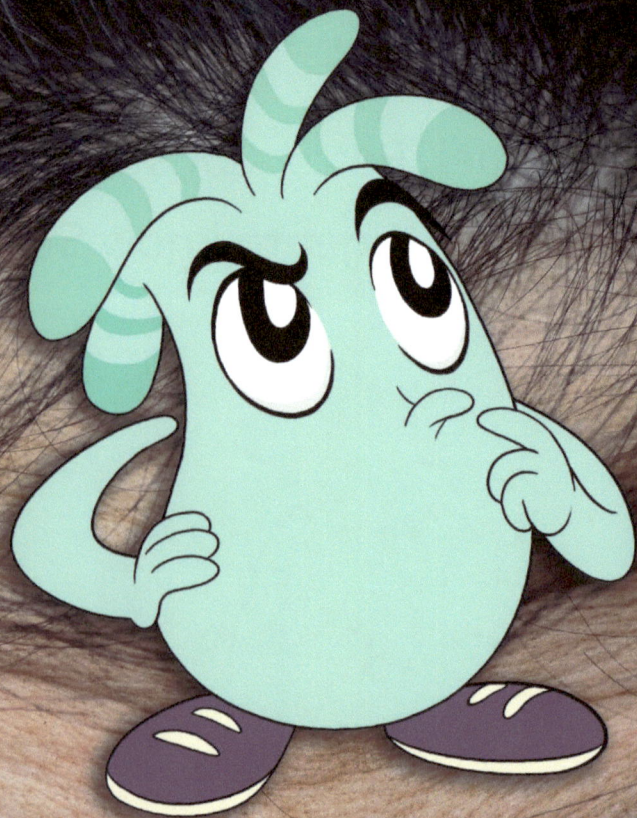

Blammo!

I woke up inside some human thing's head.

Let me tell you, there wasn't much room to spare.
I was crammed in with all these other ideas, like what to eat, when to sleep, and which big things to run from.

But hey, I'm a story!

I'm different from all the other stuff inside a human thing's head. I knew I could be a whole lot more.

So I gave the human thing a little nudge, just to see what would happen.

I gotta say, it worked!

These human things, they started to talk. Like, a lot. They did it while they were chasing things with sticks, while they chowed down, while they scratched the bug bites on their tushies...talking's a big thing with them.

Hey, I'm a story.

What can I say? I like to live out loud, so I went with it. Sometimes they *talked* about me...

... sometimes they *sang* about me, and sometimes they even *danced* about me.

Great as it was, I knew I could be more.

So I gave the human things another little poke.

It couldn't hurt, right?

It turns out these human things like to draw too. They're crazy that way.

Hey, I'm a story. I won't say no to a picture. I got scratched on cave walls, painted on rocks, and sometimes doodled on leaves and tree bark. They made carvings and sculpture things too.

Don't get me wrong, it was fantastic, but there was still more for me to be. I sent the human things a little spark.

I figured, why not?

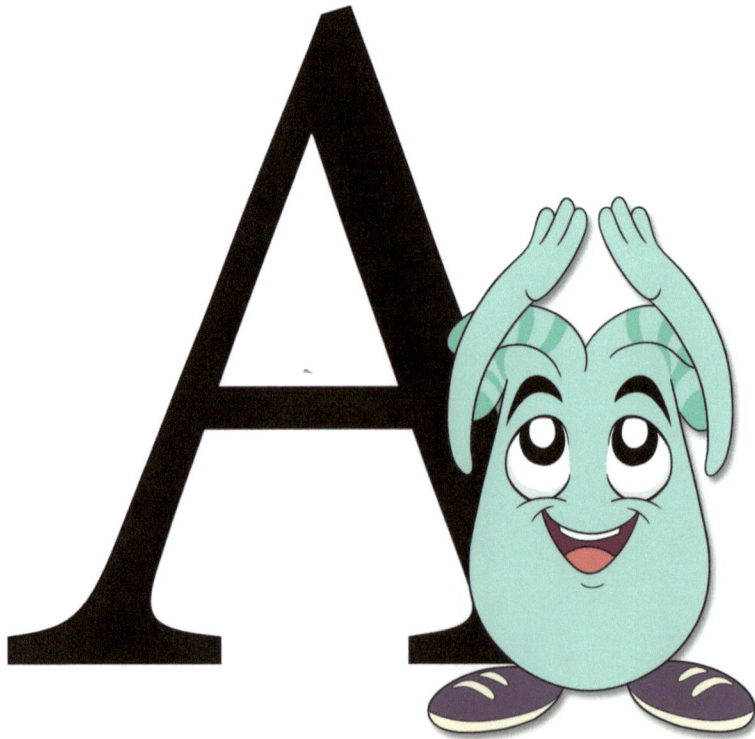

Success! The human things, they decided to make up letters, words, and sentences. They started putting all these things together.

Hey, I'm a story! I was totally on board with that!

I started showing up in writing too,
sometimes on big, flat rocks,
sometimes on these wacky wax tablets,

and then on this flat, slippery stuff the human things cooked up, called paper.

And then, get this: they figured out how to stack pieces of paper together.

They put me in these things called books!

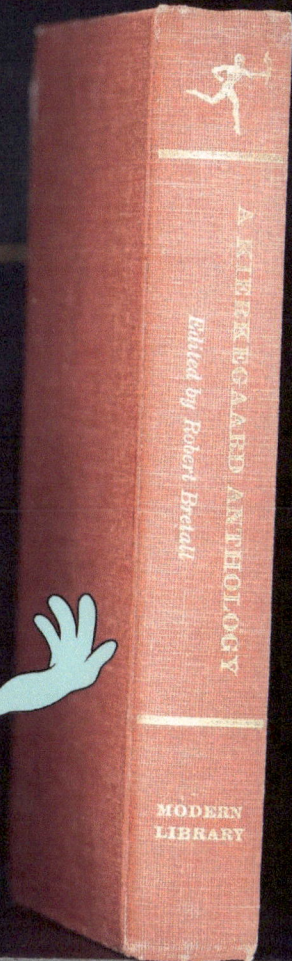

A KIERKEGAARD ANTHOLOGY

Edited by Robert Bretall

MODERN
LIBRARY

No, I'm not kidding! You can't make up stuff like this, my friends! And if you thought I would stop there, well, you've got a lot to learn about me.

Hey, I'm a story, so there's always more for me to be. I sent the human things a memo, just to keep things rolling.

How you doing? Need a pee break? Glass of water?

Go ahead. I'll wait.

All good? Now, where were we? Oh, yeah.

Remember how the human things liked to draw and carve and sculpt me? Well, I gave their brains a little tickle, and they came up with ways to make pictures that looked exactly like me.

Something about cameras, I think.

Hellooo good lookin'!

And then, get this: they found new ways to share me in sound too.

Okay, they already knew how to talk about me and sing about me.

This time around, they figured out how to blast me through the air and catch me in these little box thingies called radios.

And **ta-da!** Other human things could hear me all over the place.

Of course, I was still coming up with new things to be. I decided to toot my own horn, just to get their attention.

Aaaaaand, they took the hint.

The human things made all kinds of other gadgets and gizmos, do-whackies and thingamajigs, just so they could hear me over and over again.

No, don't get up! I'm not nearly finished!

After I dropped them another oh-so-subtle suggestion, the human things figured out how to make pictures move.

There were these movie camera things, and all kinds of screen things, and **hey, I'm a story,** so I didn't complain.

I mean, I never looked better!

Every time I figured out something else I wanted to be, human things figured out a new way to let me be it.

Every time they figured out a new way to let me be it, I figured out something else I could be.

Funny how that works, huh?

So there I was, all over the place. I was words, I was pictures, I was sounds, and I was movement.

Hey, I'm a story, so I was loving every minute of it. I mean, who wouldn't? But that doesn't mean I couldn't be more. You see where I'm going with this?

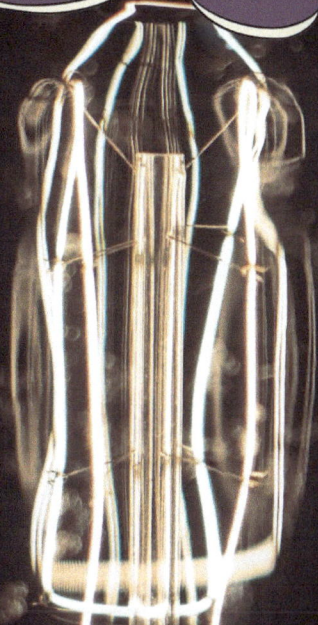

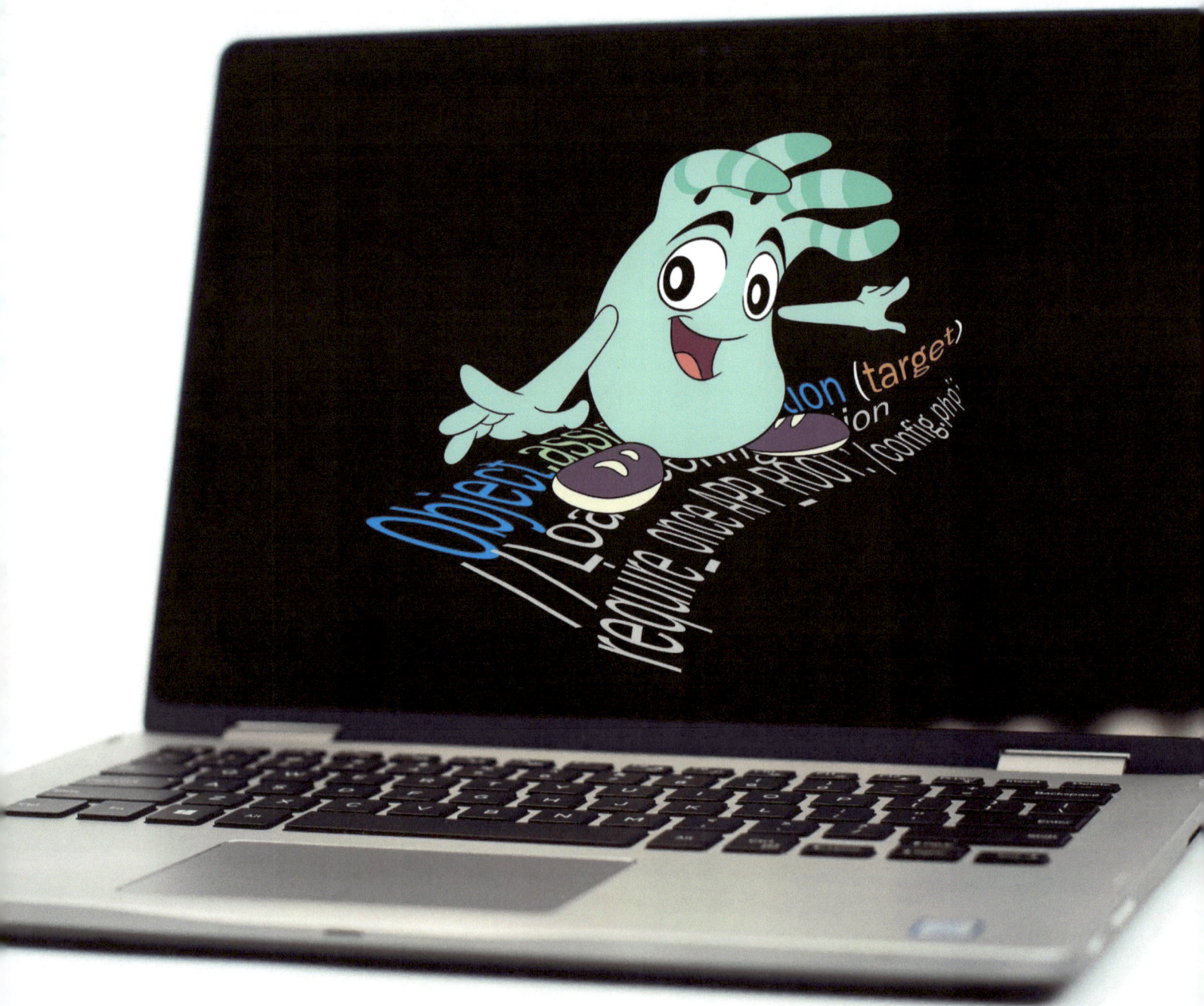

Another clue or two from me, and the human things did it again, and this time, they went big. Really, really big.

They built this web thing, something that was worldwide.

They made it so big that I could bounce all over the place, anytime a human thing wanted me. Yeah, my schedule got a little crowded, but **hey, I'm a story!**

When my fans are calling for me, I gotta show up!

Whether I was in someone's head, on a piece of paper, all lit up and making noise, or zipping all over the world, these human things couldn't get enough of me.

It was like I was part of what made them human things.

I know, right?

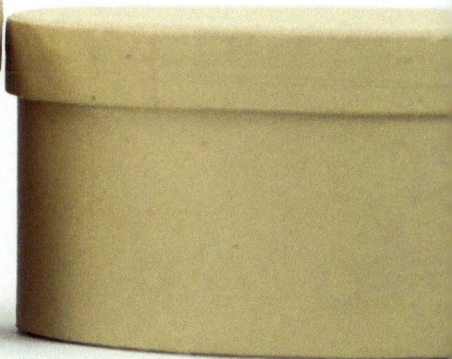

You're wondering what's next for me. Can't say I blame you. I am pretty spectacular.

Well, I still got plans to be more. That's kind of my schtick. If I know human things at all, (and after all this time, I think I do) one of them out there is figuring out some newfangled doodad to let me be me.

They're scribbling something spectacular in a notebook, or yakkity-yakking into a microphone, or wiggling their fingers over one of those screen things.

They might even be reading this book...like right now.

Hey, I'm a story.

I'm ready when you are.

You seem like a pretty smart human thing. Where do you think I'll go next? What else can I be?

Go ahead and noodle on that for a while. When you're done, there's a little extra space here for you to draw something or write something.

Just make me look good, okay?

www.ingramcontent.com/pod-product-compliance
Lightning Source LLC
Chambersburg PA
CBHW042101040426
42448CB00002B/95